SUPER FOOD
for SUPER KIDS

for Bada, my Super Kid

Joy K Hale

First U.S. paperback edition 2022

Paperback ISBN: 979-8-9865836-0-0
Hardcover ISBN: 979-8-9865836-2-4
Spanish Version ISBN: 979-8-9865836-1-7

STTL Publishing
www.sttlpublishing.com
www.SuperFoodsForSuperKids.com

An important note for parents:

This book was created to help
children become familiar with some
of the powerful nutrients inside everyday foods.

It is essential to have a balanced diet that
includes a variety of fruits, vegetables, grains,
protein, and water to help our bodies thrive.

It is my hope that this book will help kickstart
your child's interest in choosing the right foods
for a healthy lifestyle.

Joy K Hale

Did you know that some foods actually look like human body parts? Do you think there is a connection? Keep reading to find out!

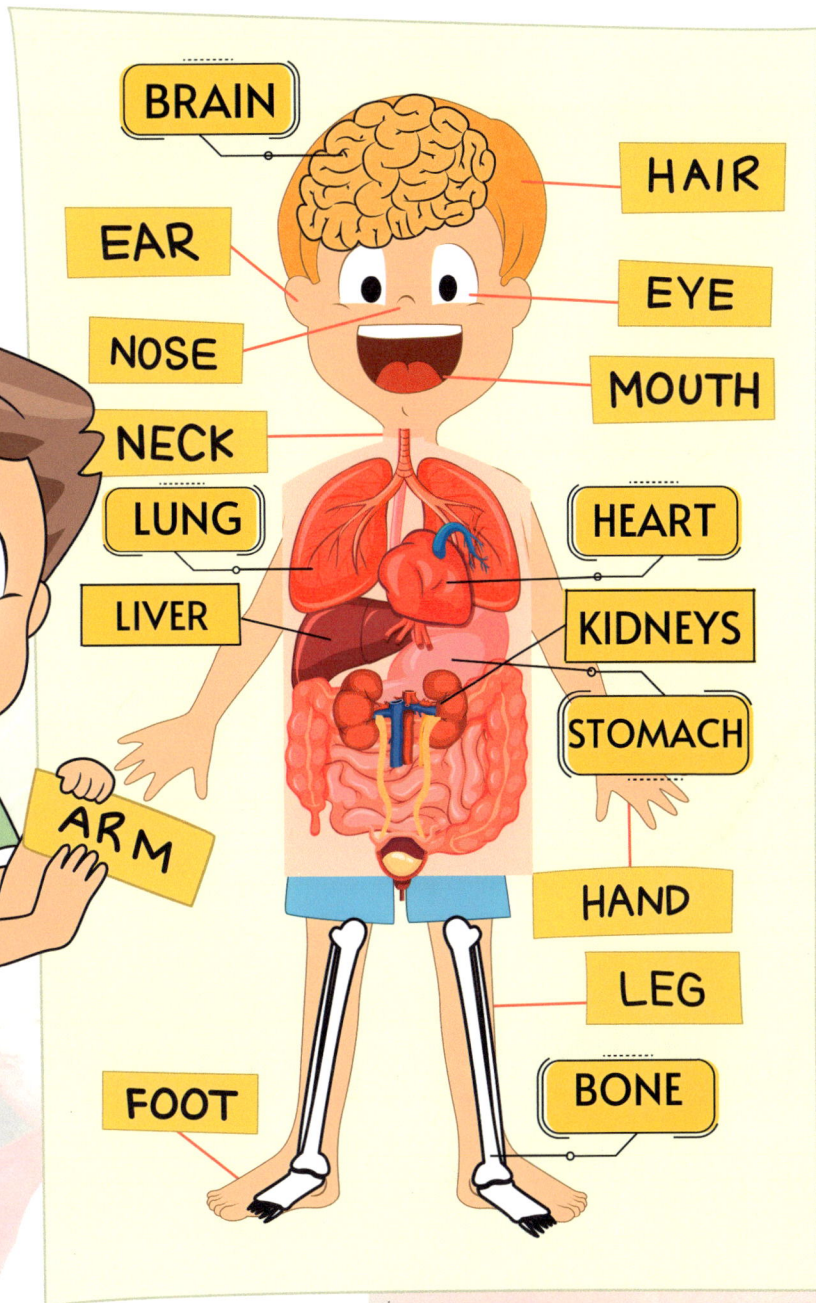

BRAIN

HAIR

EAR

EYE

NOSE

MOUTH

NECK

LUNG

HEART

LIVER

KIDNEYS

STOMACH

ARM

HAND

LEG

FOOT

BONE

Walnuts are good for your brain.

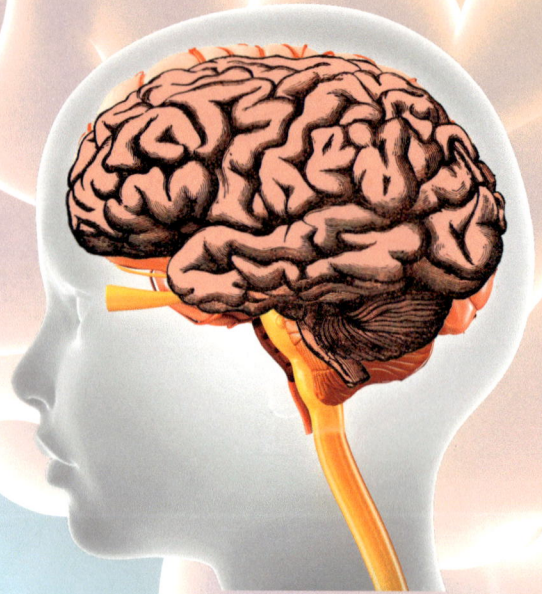

Crack open a walnut and see what is inside. It looks like a brain! A walnut and your brain both have the same shape, folds, and wrinkles.

With their high **omega-3 fatty acid** content, walnuts can help your brain to develop in a healthy way.

Carrots are good for your eyes.

Slice up a carrot and see what is inside. It looks like an eye! A carrot and your eyes both have similar circles, lines, and patterns.

With a nutrient called **beta-carotene**, carrots can help your eyes stay strong and healthy. They can help you see well even when you get older.

Pumpkin seeds are good for your nose.

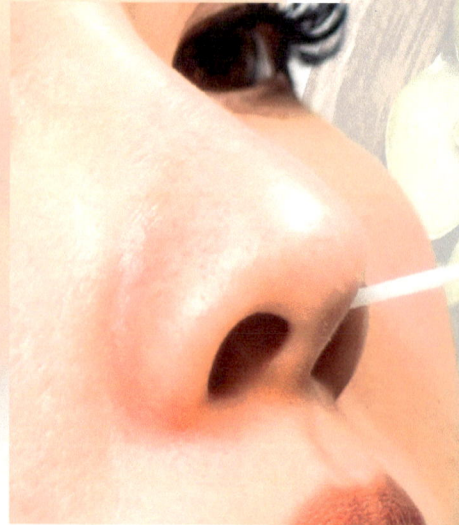

Look at a pumpkin seed. It looks like your nostril! A pumpkin seed and your nostril both have an oval shape.

With so many **vitamins** and **minerals**, pumpkin seeds can help clear a stuffy nose. Those nutrients can fight off flu symptoms, like sneezing.... achoo!

Mushrooms are good for your ears.

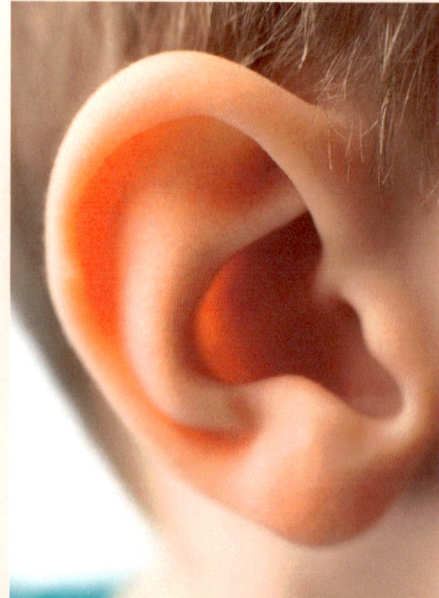

Cut a mushroom in half. It looks like your ear! A mushroom and your ear both have round curves and arched ridges.

With lots of **vitamin D,** mushrooms strengthen the small bones in your ears. This helps you to hear better and keeps your ears healthy.

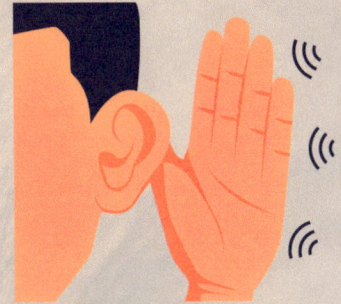

*There are over 14,000 different mushroom species with many of them being poisonous. Wild mushrooms should never be eaten unless a knowledgeable adult can first identify them to be safe.

Tomatoes are good for your heart.

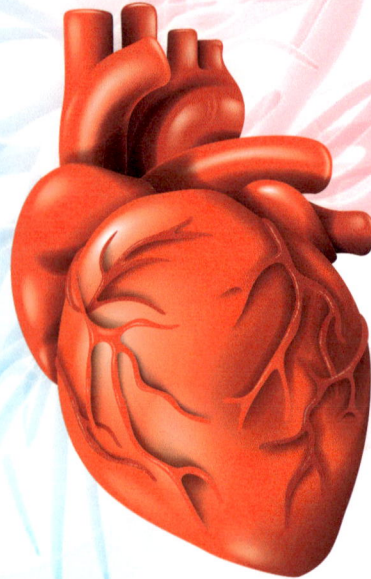

Slice a tomato and see what is inside. It looks like your heart! A tomato and your heart are both red and have multiple chambers.

With plenty of **lycopene**, tomatoes keep away heart disease and help your heart stay healthy.

Grapes are good for your lungs.

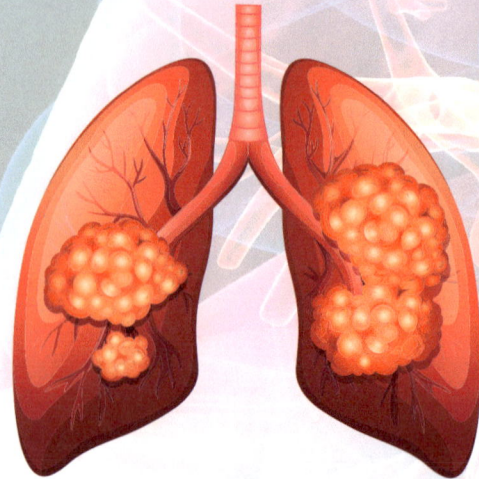

Hold up a bunch of grapes. It looks like the *alveoli* of your lungs. The *alveoli* are the tiny air sacs inside your lungs. Bunches of grapes and the *alveoli* both have the same shape and hang at the end of branches.

With lots of **_resveratrol,_** grapes can fight off bad bacteria and help us have healthy lungs.

Ginger is good for your stomach.

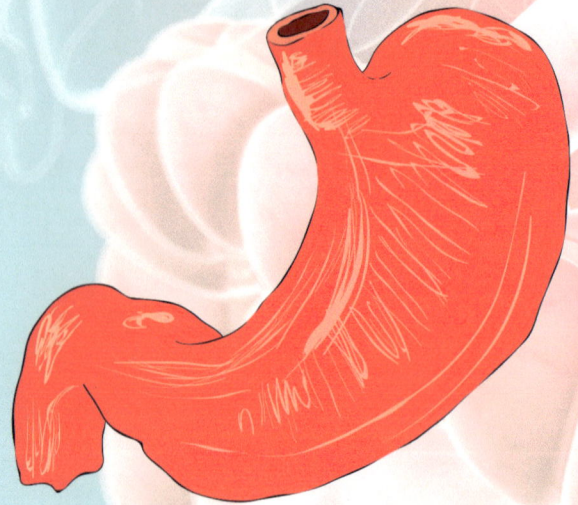

Look at a ginger root. It looks like your stomach! A ginger root and your stomach both have a curvy shape and pipes.

With lots of ***gingerols***, ginger can help your stomach digest food to make it better when it feels sick or nauseated.

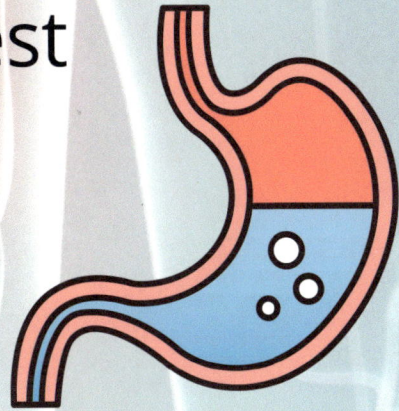

Celery is good for your bones.

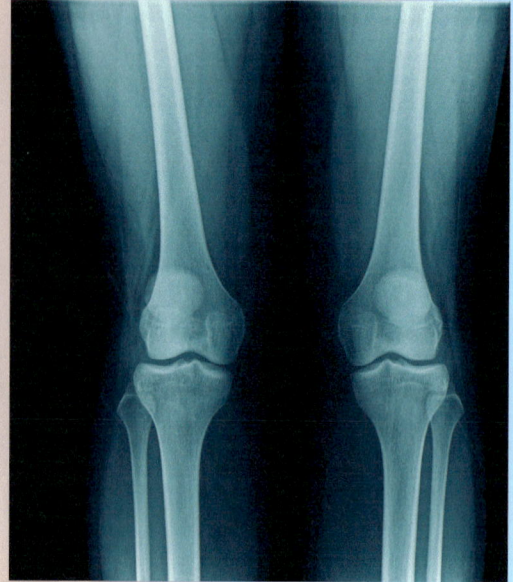

Hold up a stalk of celery. It looks like the long bones in your legs! A stalk of celery and your leg bones both are long and lean.

With lots of **silicon**, celery can help your bones grow strong.

Fun fact: Did you know that both celery and your bones contain 23% sodium?

Sweet potatoes are good for your pancreas.

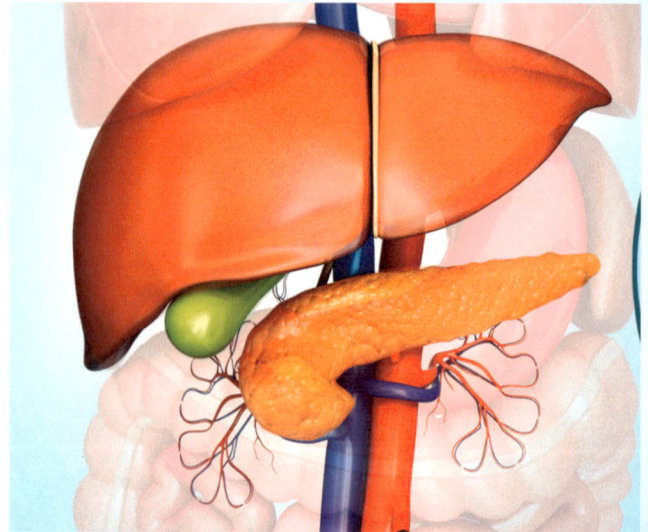

Look at a sweet potato. It looks like your pancreas! A sweet potato and your pancreas both have an oblong shape.

With lots of **antioxidants**, sweet potatoes protect your pancreas and other body tissues from disease and aging.

Kidney Beans are good for your kidneys.

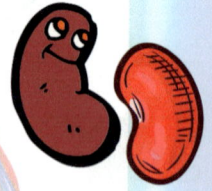

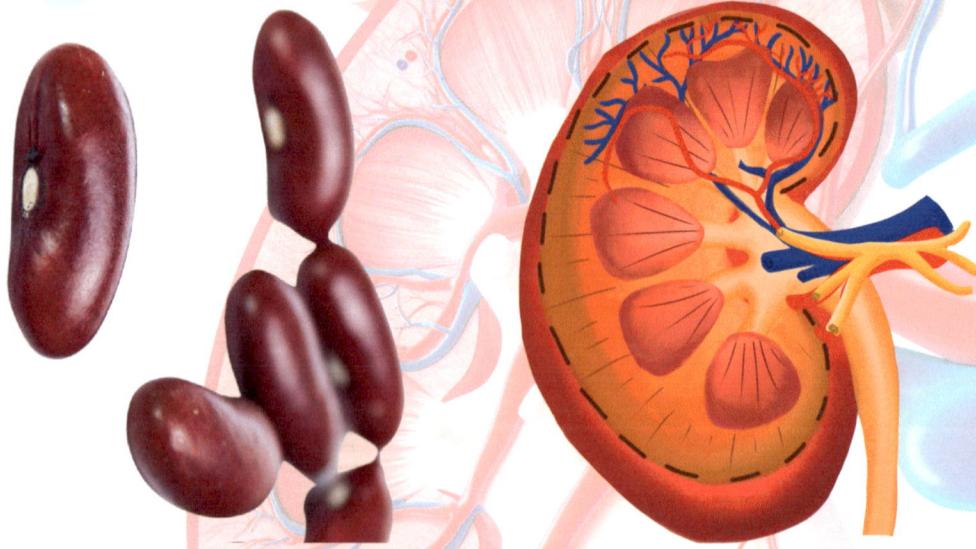

Look at a kidney bean. It is shaped exactly like your kidney- that's where the name comes from!

With many **minerals** and **vitamins**, kidney beans can help heal your kidneys and keep them strong.

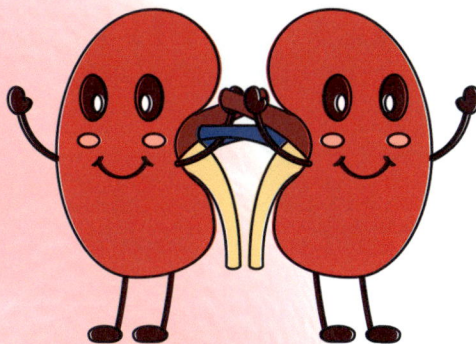

Bananas are good for your smile.

Hold up a banana.
It is shaped like your smile!

Bananas help our bodies produce a happy chemical called **serotonin**. Serotonin can help boost your positive moods and keep you feeling happy.

What other foods do you know that look like your body parts?

Can you guess which body parts these fruits and vegetables are good for?

*Scan the QR code to find out the answers!

Now we know what is good for our bodies, we can eat the right foods to stay healthy and strong together.

So eat those yummy fruits and vegetables every day to make your body SUPER!

Thank you!

Sign up to hear about free content downloads
and upcoming book launches!
You can also schedule an author visit to your school.

Visit SuperFoodsForSuperKids.com for more information.

If you enjoyed the book, we would love to hear from you!
Reviews are incredibly valuable to authors.
Please consider leaving a review on Amazon.com and
sharing a picture on social media.

#SuperFoodsForSuperKids

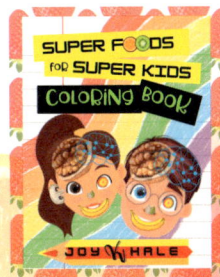

Super Foods for Super Kids Coloring Book
Also available on Amazon.com

Many of the comparisons between the foods and body parts/organs in this book are based on "the **Doctrine of Signatures** (DOS) which is a widely cited theory that purportedly explains how humans discovered the medicinal uses of some plants. According to DOS, physical characteristics of plants (including shape, color, texture, and smell) reveal their therapeutic value." (Bennett)

References

Bennett, Bradley C. American Botanical Council. Doctrine of Signatures: Through Two Millennia, 2008, www.herbalgram.org/resources/herbalgram/issues/78/

Bhavani, Ramesh T., Prem Kumar P. and Sai Krishna G. American Journal of Phytomedicine and Clinical Therapeutics. Fruits and Vegetables that Resembles to Body Organs and have Significant Role on them, 2014, www.academia.edu/6668817/

Made in United States
Troutdale, OR
09/11/2023

12815020R00021